CAVES

Troll Associates

CAVES

by Keith Brandt

Illustrated by Rex Schneider

Troll Associates

Library of Congress Cataloging in Publication Data
Brandt, Keith, (date)
   Caves.

   Summary: Describes how caves are formed and the
kinds of things one might find inside.
   1. Caves—Juvenile literature.   [1. Caves]
I. Schneider, Rex, ill.   II. Title.
GB601.2.B7   1984   551.4′47   84-2573
ISBN 0-8167-0142-3 (lib. bdg.)
ISBN 0-8167-0143-1 (pbk.)

Copyright © 1985 by Troll Associates, Mahwah, New Jersey
All rights reserved. No part of this book may be used
or reproduced in any manner whatsoever without written
permission from the publisher.
Printed in the United States of America
10   9   8   7   6   5   4   3   2   1

There is a fantastic world hidden beneath the surface of the Earth. It is the eerie home of creatures that never see the light of day. It is a world of beautiful crystals and weirdly shaped rocks, twisting tunnels and vast, domed rooms. It is a dark, silent world. It is the world of caves.

Hundreds of millions of years ago, when the Earth was young, there were no caves. In fact, the continents as we know them did not even exist. Most of North America was covered by salt water.

Living in this water were shellfish that were very much like the clams, mussels, and scallops of today. As these shellfish died, their chalky shells piled up on the ocean floor.

Millions of years passed, and the mass of shells grew thicker and heavier. Layers piled on layers, and the layers pressed down until the minerals in the shells turned to a kind of

rock called limestone. All the while this was happening, the world continued to change in other ways.

The Earth's crust shifted, and the continent of North America was pushed up where there had once been ocean. But not all the water was gone. Streams and rivers flowed over the surface, and some of this flowing water seeped into the ground.

Rain also fell and seeped into cracks in the limestone. Little by little, the waters began to eat away the rock. This was the beginning of a process that would one day carve large and small caves all over the land.

You have probably seen the way salt dissolves in water. Limestone can also dissolve, if the water dripping on it contains a mild acid. This is just what happened. The rain that fell to Earth picked up a gas called carbon dioxide from the air. And as water sank through the soil, it picked up more carbon dioxide. This carbon dioxide and water mixed chemically to become carbonic acid.

You see carbonic acid whenever you look at a bottle of soda. The bubbles in the soda are carbon dioxide. They mix with the liquid, which is mostly water, to become a weak solution of carbonic acid.

As the rainwater seeped through the limestone, the acid contained in the water began to make small holes. Centuries passed and the holes grew larger and larger. But the limestone that dissolved in the water didn't simply disappear. It flowed along with the water to different places underground. And when the water dried, the limestone was left.

In the same way, if you dissolve a spoonful of salt in a pot of water, the salt will seem to vanish. But when the water evaporates, you will see the salt again. It has been deposited on the sides and the bottom of the pot. That is just what happened to the limestone in the caves.

As the water evaporated, the limestone was deposited in different shapes. One kind of limestone deposit is long and thin and hangs like an icicle from the ceiling of a cave. It is called a *stalactite*.

A stalactite begins to form when a drop of water containing dissolved limestone seeps through to the cave's ceiling and then evaporates. A tiny bit of limestone is left there on the ceiling. Then another drop of water seeps through and evaporates in the same place. Then another, and another, and another.

As each drop of water evaporates, a bit more limestone is deposited, and the stalactite grows larger and larger. Most stalactites look something like icicles made of stone.

Sometimes a drop of water from the ceiling falls to the floor of the cave and evaporates. The limestone that was dissolved in the water is deposited on the floor. If the dripping continues, the limestone deposit grows larger and taller. After a while the deposit starts to look like an upside-down ice-cream cone. This is called a *stalagmite*.

Stalactites and stalagmites do not form overnight. Some may take 100 years to add one inch in length. Others may take only a year to add an inch.

How long it takes for stalactites and stalagmites to grow depends on several things. It depends on the amount of limestone in the rocks above the cave, the amount of water moving through the stone, and the temperatures of the rocks, air, and water. Stalactites and stalagmites form more quickly in warm conditions.

One of the world's largest and most breathtaking groups of stalactites and stalagmites is in the Carlsbad Caverns of New Mexico. In these huge caves in the southwestern United States, there are stalagmites that rise higher than a six-story building. There are ten-story high columns, formed when stalactites met stalagmites.

Limestone cave deposits may take other shapes, too. When water carrying dissolved limestone runs over cave walls and evaporates, it leaves a rippled surface called flowstone.

When water seeps through long cracks in the ceiling, the formation it leaves is called dripstone. Dripstone hangs like curtains, sometimes reaching all the way from the ceiling to the floor of the cave.

Rings of limestone may appear on the floor of the cave as water evaporates from puddles or pools. These rings are called rimstone. At the bottom of a cave pool, a grain of sand may become coated with layer upon layer of limestone, until it looks like a pearl or a marble. This is called a cave marble.

Each cave looks different from all other caves because the water that formed it contained different minerals and dripped in different ways and at different temperatures.

Where the water contained iron, cave sculptures may be red or brown or orange. Where the water contained the mineral called gypsum, the stone sculptures look like milky flower petals growing on the walls and ceilings. And where the water was free of other minerals, the limestone deposits may be in the form of clear crystals like chunks of ice or diamonds.

Not all of the world's caves are formed out of limestone. Caves along seashores are carved by the action of water on hard stone. In this case, the water isn't slowly moving water that seeps through the stone. It is fast-moving water in the form of tides, powerful waves, and wind-driven rains. A sea cave can start from just a crack in a rock. The water comes at it so often and with so much force that it hollows the rock into a large cave.

Some kinds of caves are not made by water at all. Lava caves are made from the molten rock that pours out of an erupting volcano. When the molten lava flows from the volcano, it is blisteringly hot. As it comes into contact with the air and ground, it cools and hardens.

However, if a flow of lava is thick enough, the outside cools and forms a tunnel or tube, while the lava inside stays hot and liquid. Then the molten lava flows out of the tunnel, leaving a tubelike lava cave behind it.

The walls of some lava caves are covered with ice. And some caves are made completely of ice. These ice caves were left by huge glaciers that stretched over much of the Earth millions of years ago.

Scientists say that natural caves have three zones—the *twilight zone*, the *variable-temperature zone*, and the *constant-temperature zone*.

The twilight zone goes from the mouth of the cave to as far in as daylight can reach. The temperature in the twilight zone changes with the seasons. It is a little bit cooler than the outside air in summer, and warmer than the outside air in winter. This zone is the only part of a cave where you will find green plants, such as ferns, moss, and grasses. These plants need light to grow and cannot stay alive in total darkness.

The birds, snakes, mice, skunks, and other animals found in the twilight zone are really just visitors. Caves are not their year-round homes. Some spend the winter in caves. Some use them as nests for their babies in the spring, and some use them as hiding places.

Beyond the twilight zone is the variable-temperature zone. Here, the temperature changes from winter to summer, but not as much as in the twilight zone. Plants growing in this zone are not green, since there is no sun. Only nongreen plants, such as molds and mushrooms and other fungi are found here.

The animal life of this zone includes bats, cave crickets, cave salamanders, and some fish. In the summer months, the bats roost in the cool cave during the day and fly out to hunt for insects at night. In winter, some species of bats migrate to warm climates, while other species hibernate in the cave's variable-temperature zone.

The deepest part of a cave is the constant-temperature zone. Here, the water and air stay the same temperature all year. No plant life grows here, and the animal life is very strange.

The lobsterlike, cave-dwelling crayfish has no eyes, is thin, milky white, and very slow moving. Its brightly colored relatives who live outside the cave have bulging eyes, are larger, and faster moving. Other creatures of the constant-temperature zone, such as cave crickets, beetles, fish, and worms, are also blind and colorless.

People have lived in caves, too, since prehistoric times. But they always stayed fairly close to the entrance. And, like the frogs and birds and small animals that spend part of the time in caves, people have used caves as part-time shelter, leaving them to hunt and fish. We know about these long-ago cave-dwellers from the evidence they left behind them in the caves.

In France and Spain, there are caves with beautiful paintings of deer and horses, birds and fish, and human beings. In North America, wall paintings and colorful reed baskets have been found in caves. And in other places in the world, scientists have found bones, pottery, stone tools, and other signs of long-ago human existence.

Yet even though people have been using them for hundreds of thousands of years, caves continue to keep many mysteries buried in their dark, twisting passages. And caves continue to be a fascinating world of beauty and adventure.